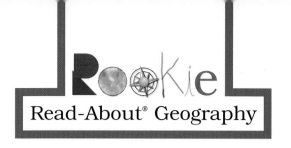

Read-About® Geography

Living on a Prairie

By Jan Mader

Consultant
Nanci R. Vargus, Ed.D.
Assistant Professor of Literacy
University of Indianapolis
Indianapolis, Indiana

Children's Press®
A Division of Scholastic Inc.
New York   Toronto   London   Auckland   Sydney
Mexico City   New Delhi   Hong Kong
Danbury, Connecticut

Designer: Herman Adler Design
Photo Researcher: Caroline Anderson
The photo on the cover shows a farm on a prairie in South Dakota.

Library of Congress Cataloging-in-Publication Data

Mader, Jan.
  Living on a prairie / by Jan Mader.
     p. cm. — (Rookie read-about geography)
  Summary: A brief introduction to prairies, describing where they are located
  in the United States, the plants and animals found there, and how their use
  has changed over the years.
     ISBN 0-516-22756-4 (lib. bdg.)   0-516-25932-6 (pbk.)
     1. Prairie ecology—United States—Juvenile literature. 2. Prairies—United
  States—Juvenile literature. [1. Prairies.] I. Title. II. Series.
     QH104.M28 2004
     577.4'4—dc22
                                        2003016934

CHILDREN'S PRESS, and ROOKIE READ-ABOUT®,
and associated logos are trademarks and or registered trademarks
of Scholastic Library Publishing. SCHOLASTIC and associated logos
are trademarks and or registered trademarks of Scholastic Inc.

1 2 3 4 5 6 7 8 9 10 R 13 12 11 10 09 08 07 06 05 04

What is made of grass and looks almost like an ocean?

A prairie does.

Prairies are large, flat areas of land that are covered in grasses.

When the wind blows, these grasses can look like waves.

6

There are very few trees on a prairie. Some prairies have low bushes.

Most prairies have pretty wildflowers.

Another name for a prairie
is a grassland.

Many different kinds of
grass grow on a prairie.
The grasses can grow tall.

9

Summers on a prairie are very hot. Winters are very cold and snowy.

The spring and fall are
sometimes rainy.

Prairie dogs live on
the prairie.

Prairie dogs are not really
dogs. They are rodents
like mice and squirrels.

They dig tunnels in the
ground and eat the grasses.

Prairie dogs

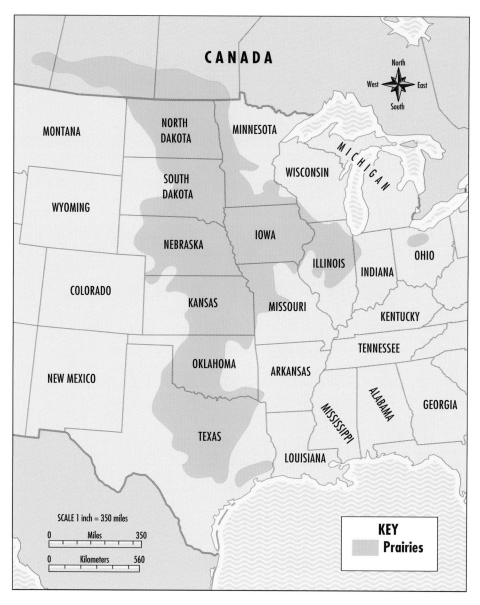

KEY
Prairies

SCALE 1 inch = 350 miles

| | Miles | |
| 0 | | 350 |

| | Kilometers | |
| 0 | | 560 |

14

Prairies reach all the way from Texas to northern Canada.

Can you count how many states have prairies?

Many years ago, prairies covered much of the land in the Midwestern United States.

There were no buildings or farms. There were just miles and miles of prairie.

Some groups of Native Americans lived on the prairie.

They used the plants to make medicines. They hunted the bison and other prairie animals for food.

Then, new settlers came.
They crossed the prairies
in large wagons called
prairie schooners.

The settlers plowed the
land, and planted wheat
and corn.

A ranch

Today there is not much open prairie left. Instead, there are towns, farms, and ranches.

Ranch animals eat the grasses that grow on the prairie.

Look at this big city. It was built on prairie land.

Many of the people who live here work in offices. Others work in stores and factories.

Bison

Some people want to have more open prairie again. They are planting new prairie grasses and flowers.

They are making sure that bison and other prairie animals have places to live.

What do you like best about prairies?

Words You Know

bison

grasses

prairie dogs

30

prairie schooners

ranch

wildflowers

31

Index

About the Author

Jan Mader has been writing children's books for over 15 years. Her natural curiosity and joy of life characterize her work. Jan loves to ride her horses, Tango and Piper, through the tall grasses on the open prairie.

Photo Credits

Photographs © 2004: Bridgeman Art Library International Ltd., London/New York/Indianapolis Museum of Art, USA: 17; Corbis Images: 25 (Bruce Burkhardt), 22, 31 bottom left (Royalty-Free); Dembinsky Photo Assoc.: 13, 30 bottom right (Claudia Adams), 6, 31 bottom right (Willard Clay), 5, 30 bottom left (Gary Meszaros), 3 (G. Alan Nelson), 26, 30 top (Alan G. Nelson); Greg Ryan/Sally Beyer: 21, 31 top; Photo Researchers, NY: 10 (Rod Planck), 9 (Jim Steinberg); PictureHistory.com: 18; Stone/Getty Images: cover; Superstock, Inc.: 29; Tom Bean: 11.

Map by Bob Italiano